FLOWER GARDENING

FLOWER GARDENING

Ethne Clarke

WITH A FOREWORD BY
MAX DAVIDSON

SUNBURST BOOKS

This edition first published in 1996 by
Sunburst Books,
Deacon House,
65 Old Church Street,
London SW3 5BS.

ISBN 1 85778 169 4

Publishing Manager *Casey Horton*
Design Manager *Ming Cheung*
Editor *Jennifer Spaeth*
Designer *Sean Bennett*

Publisher's Note
Readers should note that plant breeders introduce new cultivars all the time.
Please check your seed catalogues for the latest ones.

WARNING
If using chemical herbicides,
fungicides or insecticides, be sure to
follow exactly the manufacturer's
instructions

Printed in Hong Kong

CONTENTS

FOREWORD

With the huge choice of flowers available today our gardens can be almost permanently in bloom. Patios, window boxes and the tiniest of gardens have long relied on the annuals and biennials to provide colour, but one of the major changes in the way we cultivate our gardens has been the move in recent years to perennial plants.

In the past the herbaceous border was regarded as the preserve of large houses. The plants were carefully graded in rows according to their heights and carefully staked.

It was all very time-consuming and unnecessary. The herbaceous border has made a comeback in a much more relaxed and informal guise. No more do the borders have to be backed by clipped hedges or flanked by large expanses of well-cut turf or a gravel path.

Today's herbaceous plants are often grown in quite small island beds surrounded by lawn, so that we can enjoy all of the plants to the full.

The current thinking in the gardening world is to keep staking to a minimum, so plants such as the many varieties of the popular herbaceous geranium can be allowed to sprawl as they will. We are also seeing the resurgence of interest in kniphofias and euphorbias – both plants give a solid structure to any bed.

When herbaceous borders relied heavily on plants such as lupins, irises and delphiniums they were rightly regarded as two-week wonders of early summer. But now a well-planned herbaceous bed, with carefully chosen plants, can provide colorful flowers constantly from early spring until late autumn.

The structure of the border is also less rigid than it once was, since modern herbaceous borders can have the added attraction of bush roses and the occasional shrub.

Thanks to the great scientific strides which have been made in flower breeding, the standard annual now blooms better and longer than ever before. The mainstay for autumn and winter is the pansy, which opens its face to the sun during mild spells. Spring gives us the chance to enjoy some superb primroses and polyanthus in every colour of the rainbow. In summer we have the brilliant shades of the petunias and busy lizzies to fill containers with colour that lasts until the first frosts.

For adventurous gardeners there are, of course, many more flowers which can be raised from seed. Sowing seeds and raising your own plants on the windowsill, if you don't have a greenhouse, is one of the most satisfying of gardening enterprises.

Gardening was once mainly about growing fruits and vegetables, but today, as so many gardens have become smaller, the move is distinctly towards flowers – from the first white snowdrops of winter to the fireworks of autumn in the form of red, pink and purple Michaelmas daisies. By planting the wide range of bulbs and perennials, which are readily available from garden centres and nurseries, and sowing seeds annually in spring we can have colour all year.

So look on your garden as a canvas and apply bold brushstrokes of floral colour to give it life and interest in every season.

Max Davidson

INTRODUCTION

Of all the types of gardening you can undertake – vegetable and fruit, rock and alpine, green-house and so on – flower gardening is in many ways the most satisfyingly creative. In a flower garden you are an artist working with the textures and shapes of flowers and leaves from a colourful palette.

The earliest flower gardens were the simple rectangular beds

within the monastic cloister where, alongside herbs and vegetables, the monks cultivated a range of simple flowers to decorate the altar and make garlands for holy days. From these purely functional plots evolved the ornamental garden, where flowers were grown for their decorative value and for inspiring the heart and souls of troubadours, knights and their ladies with thoughts of perfect love. The flowery mead was a simple lawn within the confines of the castle precincts where noble ladies and their retinue would while away their time. Manuscript illuminations from the 15th century give us glimpses of these enclosed gardens. Bounded by simple, wooden trellis fences and carpeted with camomile lawns, there was most often a single central fruit tree, perhaps garlanded with honeysuckle. The lawn was dotted with marguerites and the common lawn daisy, and simple bulbs such as daffodils and bluebells, Alba roses (among the oldest in cultivation), madonna lilies, thyme and rosemary grew in profusion. Whatever flowers there were, they were always the uncomplicated herbs and shrubs of the hedgerow and meadow, for this was well before the idea of plant breeding and the introduction of New World plants, which followed the European discovery of the Americas at the turn of the 16th century, and opened the portals to the world of flower gardening as we know it today.

Flowers reigned supreme for several centuries until the late 17th century. Through most of the 18th century the art of gardening became a pursuit of 'improving nature'. William Kent and Capability Brown were the master plantsmen of

their day, and their designs banished flower gardens from view to be replaced by landscape gardens. These were carefully contrived, 'natural' landscaped parks of inspiring vistas, newly planted 'ancient' woodlands and sublime lakes and streams constructed by a huge workforce (often composed of displaced villagers whose homes had been obliterated to make way for the vista – such are the things that have been done in the name of art!).

But all was not lost for the flower gardener; in the simple country garden of the yeomen farmers and land-owning gentry, beds of roses, lilies, marguerites and hollyhocks thrived and awaited revival by the following generations. Gertrude Jekyll was their champion and during the late Victorian and early Edwardian period the revival of the cottage garden was her special campaign.

Jekyll was a watercolourist by training, a craftswoman at heart and perfectionist by nature, and these qualities were combined to create some of the most influential planting schemes ever created for flower gardens. Her writings about gardening have also had a lasting impact, none more so than *Colour Schemes for the Flower Garden*, which is available today in a reprint edition. If you are serious about your flower gardening it is well worth reading, if only to inform you about what makes many contemporary garden designers tick.

The preceding paragraphs are just a glimpse at the fascinating history of one aspect of gardening. Today flower gardening is taking a more ecological tilt, with much more emphasis on growing plants in self-sustaining groups selected according to their mutual compatibility for soil and climate conditions. Where Jekyll-style gardeners find their balance in colour harmonies, eco-gardeners strive for a balance of nature.

Perhaps gardeners have never before had such a large playing field, which makes it all the more important to choose your game and understand the rules before you begin to play.

PREPARING THE GARDEN

WHEN PREPARING A GARDEN YOU SHOULD consider the soil and site first because the conditions provided there will influence the type of plants you grow, no matter what style you choose to arrange them in the garden.

Soil and Site

One of the single most important factors in flower gardening is knowing the degree of alkalinity of the garden soil. Some plants hate alkaline conditions, which are found in chalky soils, and so require acid conditions such as those found in peaty soils. Rhododendrons, azaleas and heathers are the best examples of acid-loving plants. To find out what type of soil you have you must test the soil's pH using a meter that has a probe, which you simply poke into the soil, or else with a special indicator fluid that is mixed with the soil. The fluid will cause a colour change, which is read against a chart. The pH is measured on a scale of 0–14 – the higher the number, the more alkaline the soil. Most garden soil reads between 5 and 8, so 7 is regarded as neutral. A pH of 6.5, however, is thought to be the most ideal as it suits the widest range of plants.

On the whole it is better to avoid the frustration of trying to grow acid-loving plants in alkaline soil and vice versa, but if you simply must have acid-loving plants such as rhododendrons or lavender, then you can dig in plenty of peat and use a high-acid fertiliser such as sulphate of ammonia, or apply an acid-releasing compound.

Acid soils can be amended and made more alkaline by adding garden lime during late winter, but don't do it at the same time as you are digging in manure or compost: generally, 450 g/1 lb of ground limestone to a sq m/sq yd will raise the pH of ordinary garden soil by about one point. Sandy soil will need half this amount: heavy clay, half as much again.

The flower garden or border should be prepared several months ahead of planting, beginning work in the autumn if possible. Dig the soil as deeply as you can; the ideal is to dig to a depth of twice the depth of the

ABOVE: Soil testing will help you to choose the plants best suited to your garden site.

RIGHT: A cottage-style garden is one of loose informality, where flowers of all types grow in harmony.

8

LEFT: Digging-in flower beds is one of the first steps in preparing a flower garden.

BELOW: Every season has its colours; spring is soft and pastel, while autumn blazes with the vibrant colours of half-hardy plants such as the dahlias and phlox shown here.

blade of the spade. Next, dig in as much well-rotted manure or garden compost as you can no matter what sort of soil you have. All this is hard work, but the more effort you put into the preparation the better, as the plants will then benefit from ideal growing conditions.

Dress the soil with bone meal several weeks before planting and in the following spring apply a balanced fertiliser such as NPK, which has equal percentages of nitrogen, phosphorus and potash; each of these elements benefits a different part of the plant's development. Application rates will have been calculated by the manufacturer and these should be followed to avoid over-use.

Many of the plants you will want to grow will do well in a wide variety of positions around the garden as long as they have properly prepared soil and at least a few hours of good sunlight for part of the day. There are plants, of course, that prefer full shade and others which demand full sun, but any good nurseryman should be able to provide you with information about cultivation for individual plants.

Planning the Planting

Most flower gardens contain a great many more perennials than any other group of plants, but it is a good idea to incorporate a few evergreen and deciduous shrubs, such as holly, box, lilacs, hydrangeas and shrub roses to give structure and substance to the flower garden scheme. Annuals and biennials are also useful to include in your planning since these temporary residents will fill in any gaps in the planting, while the permanent residents (perennials and shrubs) are becoming established. Annuals and biennials are also good at playing the stop-gap, making a bridge of colour between perennial flowering seasons.

ABOVE: Buddleia and echinops are both good butterfly plants.

BELOW: Topiary shapes, such as these bold cones, give structure to a border.

PLANT GROUPS

Herbaceous perennials are plants that thrive for between three and five years, although there are exceptions, such as peonies, which live far longer. The top growth (the part of the plant above the soil) of herbaceous perennials dies down during the winter when the roots and crowns remain dormant underground and send up fresh shoots in spring. Hardy perennials survive the winter unprotected in the border; tender perennials do not, however, and should be lifted and stored under cover or else propagated by cuttings in late summer to be planted out the following spring after the last frost.

Evergreens are also perennials, but they retain their leaves throughout the winter. Most are shrubs and live longer than the herbaceous flowering perennials. Don't be fooled by the name – some evergreens have stunning grey foliage.

Deciduous shrubs have a permanent framework of woody stems and lose their leaves during winter.

Annuals complete their entire life cycle all within a single season, usually in the same year, with seed sown in spring, flowering in summer and setting seed before dying in the autumn. There are a number of hardy annuals that survive frost, and so can be sown in autumn to flower a little

LEFT: **There are many ways to organise plants in a garden scheme. Here, spring-flowering herbaceous perennials and shrubs are grouped together for a seasonal display.**

earlier the following year than seed that is sown in the spring. Half-hardy annuals are killed by frost, so must be sown when there is no risk of frost or else in warmth either on a kitchen windowsill or in a greenhouse, then grown on protected from frost, and planted out in early summer.

Biennials germinate one year, flower the next and then die. Some biennials, such as sweet williams, will flower the first year if sown early enough in the season and are therefore treated as annuals.

A word of caution about buying perennials and shrubs from garden centres and DIY chains: plants are living things and without proper care in their juvenile years will suffer disease and stunted growth. Most centres take great care of their plant stocks – they amount to a serious investment after all – and they see that while the plants are on their staging they are kept watered, well-lit or shaded as required by the plant and, of course, weed and pest free. These are the plants to look for. Avoid purchasing plants that are yellowed or have withered growing tips, that have roots growing through the drainage holes on the bottom of the container or that have colonies of lichens and mosses growing on the surface of the potting compost. Rescue missions are possible, and some gardeners I know seem to treat their borders as convalescent homes for ailing plants, but it is far better to start as you mean to carry on, with healthy stock in a well-prepared and healthy environment. Does the plant have a good, balanced shape? Are there plenty of emerging buds indicating the potential for vigorous new growth? These are other things to look for.

Many of the plants we purchase today are container-grown, and the theory is that they can be planted at almost anytime of year, as long as the ground is not frozen or there is not a drought. However, it is best to do the main planting in autumn or spring, so the plants have time to put down new roots and settle in before the activity of the growing season. If it is not possible to do the majority of the planting all at one time, you can plant at other times, but then take care to water well or mulch for frost protection. Annuals and biennials are all easily home-grown from seed, but you can also buy annual bedding plants in the spring and biennials in the autumn.

ABOVE: Annuals are the mainstay of summer bedding.

BELOW: A typical cottage garden scene with a rose-covered pergola underplanted with salvia, hemerocallis, alchemilla, geranium and centaurea.

Designing the Flower Garden

The main thing to keep in mind is that this is your garden and you are designing it for your pleasure and to your tastes, not to what some garden pundit might dictate. If you like bedding plants in bright colours and geometric patterns – go for it. If you want to create a Jekyll-style, colour-led planting, where every single flower has its role to play in manipulating the visual senses – do it. In my own flower garden I have tried to arrange my flower borders according to the seasons, as each season has its own particular colour themes. So the early spring border of pale blues and soft yellows moves into the warmer summer border with shades of velvet red old roses, faded foxglove pink, lavender purples and silver foliage, deepening as winter closes in with an autumnal border of Michaelmas daisies, bronze grasses and vividly coloured autumn crocus. This is just one way of ordering the flowers about.

It is often written that tall plants should go to the back of the border, medium-height plants to the centre and low growers kept to the front. I prefer to mix them up, so that tall, wiry-stemmed plants can be at the front, making a screen of colour and texture through which the lower-growing subjects at the back are viewed. I don't cut down my plants the minute they fade; I leave some to seed about and others to add their changing, fading foliage to the colour panoply. It makes for a shaggy garden, but that is what suits me.

If you have trouble defining your style, take a look through one of the many garden style books on the market, as well as at the photos in this book. Make a note of what takes your fancy and of plants that particularly catch your eye. You should also visit as many gardens as you can; one of the best ways of learning how to garden is by talking to other gardeners – it is also one of gardening's greatest pleasures.

PLANTING AND PLANT MAINTENANCE

IT IS PROBABLY A GOOD IDEA to make a sketch of the planting plan before you begin, if only to give some order to your thoughts. When you finally step into the garden to begin the actual work of putting plant in soil, you may find that reality takes over from dream and the whole thing changes, but that is life. Try to achieve a balance of foliage, flower, height and colour. The fading foliage of early flowering plants may need screening by late-flowering subjects; evergreens dotted through the scheme will help to keep interest going through the barren months of winter.

Choose a bright, open, sunny autumn day to do the planting – one which may well be followed by a few rainy days is ideal (it helps to be psychic) – and set the plants out in the borders, according to your design. This will help you to see if you have chosen the right plants, that they are correctly spaced and that you have enough to make the planting effective. Try to plant perennials in groups of three, five or seven, rather than as lonesome individuals. Remove the plants from their containers one at a time as they are planted, so if you don't finish the job all at once the remaining plants will still be safely potted.

Treat the plants carefully and check the rootball – if the roots are all coiled around each other, gently tease a few of them out by scratching at them with the tips of your fingers. Dig out a hole larger than the diameter of the root ball, but not much deeper, so that you are planting the crown just below soil level.

Plants ordered by post will usually arrive with their roots wrapped in damp paper and polythene. Take the plants from the packing case, but leave the roots securely wrapped to keep them moist until you are ready to plant them out. These plants should have their roots spread out, so the soil backfill can be firmed around them. If bad weather or lack of time prevents you from planting bare-rooted plants for more than two days, the roots should be covered by moist peat and the plants tucked away in a shady spot until you can do the planting.

At planting time, if the ground is dry, fill the planting hole with water and let it seep away before you put the plant in position. This is called puddling-in. After planting, water well in order to give enough water to soak the roots. If it does not rain within a few days of planting, water by

ABOVE: **Wait until the danger of frost is past before planting bedding plants in the border.**

RIGHT: **Standard buxus is a good shrub for topiary training; clipping is usually done in July.**

14

LEFT: **Planting herbaceous plants can continue from winter to spring.**

hand. If the weather is particularly dry you might have to do this every day until the plants are established.

Hardy annuals and biennials can be sown where they are to flower; half-hardy annuals and hardy bedding plants that you have purchased from the nursery are planted as herbaceous perennials. Bulbs and corms are normally planted in holes twice the depth of the bulb (5 cm/2 in of soil above a bulb 2.5 cm/1 in deep). If you are unable to plant immediately, keep them in moist peat.

Keeping the Plants Going

Once the plants are in place in the border, they must be tended to regularly; you cannot just leave them to their own devices. If you did, they would soon grow woody, cease to flower or become diseased, through overcrowding and lack of good soil nutrients. The simple practices that are needed to maintain healthy plants and a beautiful garden follow.

BELOW: **Only water the garden when it is absolutely necessary; routine watering can be detrimental to plants.**

MULCHING

A mulch can be made from well-rotted manure, compost, chipped bark or coir. Many past generations of gardeners relied on moss peat for mulching flower beds, but in the past decade it has been recognised that the stripping of peat bogs was destroying a virtually unrenewable natural resource – it takes millennia for a peat bog to evolve.

Mulching helps to suppress weed growth, as a properly laid mulch – one which covers the surface of the soil to a depth of at least 7.5 cm/3 in – hinders seed germination; any weeds which do take hold are also much

easier to pull from the soil. A mulch should be applied in spring when the soil is moist and beginning to warm up; later in the season the mulch will prevent the soil drying out. When laying the mulch, don't put it right up against the base of the plant, as this can damage emerging shoots.

WATERING

Most of your watering efforts should be concentrated on newly planted subjects, especially if the weather is dry or windy. When you water be sure to do so thoroughly, since a light sprinkle will draw roots to the surface where they will be more likely to suffer from drought or dying wind. Moisture-loving plants should have special treatment during dry spells to ensure they receive adequate water.

STAKING

Some tall-growing perennials need support from stakes, canes, peasticks or twiggy branches (hazel branches are much used for this). There are also a number of wire supports on the market; these are expensive but they do last a long time. Always put supports in place as the plants are coming into growth; that way they will be disguised by the mature foliage and flowers of the plants.

BELOW: **A frame of twigs supports sweet peas. Not only is it beneficial for the plant's growth, but it is also pleasing to the eye.**

WEEDING

Not only does a weed-choked border look a mess, but the weeds will also compete with the ornamental plants for food and moisture – and the weeds will most likely win, stunting growth and weakening your precious flowers. Perennial weeds can be painted with herbicide solutions, since it is difficult to spray in a border without harming neighbouring plants, but regular hoeing is far and away the most effective weed control system.

DEAD-HEADING AND CUTTING BACK

Regular removal of faded flower heads will help prolong the flowering period by conserving the plant's energy and postponing seed production. In the case of bulbs, it helps to conserve their strength and quality of the bulb. However, some plants should be left to seed – I like to leave bronze fennel, many hardy annuals and some of the best species perennials to set seed. Nature has a way of putting self-sown seedlings in just the right places, and it is an inexpensive way of increasing stocks of particular plants. For example, I have carpets of hardy cyclamen and a mass of hostas from self-sown plants. Also, some seed heads can be exceedingly pretty and contribute to the beauty of the autumn flower garden. When dead-heading use scissors or secateurs if the stem is tough, otherwise just pinch off the flower heads.

In late winter or early spring, it will be time to cut back the withered stems and spent seed heads of herbaceous perennials; this process helps to tidy the border for the coming season. Cut the dead material to within 10 cm/4 in of the base.

ABOVE: Regular hoeing is the most thorough way to control weeds. Hoe when the weather is dry and warm.

LEFT: Dead-heading will help to prolong the flowering season by preventing seed production.

RIGHT: Rust disfigures lupin and foliage of other plants.

BELOW: Blackfly will eventually sap the strength of infested plants, withering flowering stems and destroying plants.

Pests and Diseases

Slugs, snails, greenfly, blackfly, black spot, rust, mildew and birds: the list of bugs and ailments that can strike the flower garden is seemingly endless, and there are few gardeners who are spared the routines of spraying and dusting in an effort to keep the garden healthy. On the whole, the best treatment is prevention: keep the flowerbeds free of fallen leaves, faded petals and other debris that might harbour pests, and feed and water adequately – a well-grown plant is a healthy plant and one more able to resist infection. If in spite of your best efforts the plants are attacked, you can go to their defence with any number of chemicals applied as sprays or dusts. General-purpose insecticides include malathion, derris, pyrethrum and a host of other compounds. Useful fungicides are benomyl and mancozeb. Manufacturers take great care with their labelling, so read the information provided thoroughly and follow dosage instructions to the letter. The only diseases that can not be effectively treated are virus induced. Contorted stems, blotched leaves and deformed growth indicate a virus and the only thing to do is dig up the plant and burn it.

WARNING: Garden chemicals have toxic properties and many are also irritants; in some countries these are clearly labelled as such with a large black 'X' on the packaging. Keep all chemicals in their original containers – do not decant into soda water bottles or other containers, from which a child might be tempted to drink; wear protective clothing, masks and goggles when using and never spray on windy days.

Raising Your Own Plants

GARDEN CENTRES AND NURSERIES are valuable hunting grounds for new plants and for seasonal supplies of annuals. However, you must not forget that you can get a lot of pleasure from propagating your own stocks, with the added benefit of saving money at the same time.

Seed-sowing

There are few things more rewarding than watching a tiny seed mature into a stunning plant. Success with seed sowing depends entirely on keeping the seedlings moist, warm and provided with adequate light. Patience is also required, but the outcome is worth the wait.

HARDY ANNUALS AND BIENNIALS

These plants should be sown where they are meant to flower. Sow hardy annuals in spring or early autumn and biennials during the summer. Make shallow drills with a cane, water the drill and then scatter the seed thinly along the drill. Don't make straight lines in flowerbeds; instead draw curving drills in and around herbaceous plants. Alternatively, you can sow the seed in patches to give a clumping effect. Lightly rake the soil over the seed and water the drill with a watering can fitted with a fine rose. Make sure the soil is kept moist until the seedlings begin to emerge. Thin the plants when they have developed their first true leaves by removing the weakest growing plants to ensure that the plants are spaced far enough apart to allow for healthy growth. Biennials can also be sown on a nursery bed to be trans-planted during autumn or the following spring.

ABOVE: Young plants of annuals growing in a frame in early summer for planting out later in the season.

RIGHT: Cottage garden flowers for summer include sunflowers, verbascum and cornflowers: all can be given a head start by raising seed indoors.

HALF-HARDY ANNUALS

These types of plants are usually sown in seed trays or pots, then placed in warmth – either in a propagator in the greenhouse or on a windowsill indoors – in late winter or early spring; the seed packet will advise you about sowing times. As soon as the seedlings have developed their first true leaves they should be pricked out, which means transplanted, into

20

trays of fresh compost or else into individual cells or pots. There are a few systems on the market, including peat plugs, where the seed is sown into each pot, which is then watered to expand the plug. The seedlings are thinned in the plug and then grown on to plant out when ready. This process avoids pricking out, which is an occasion for disease to attack and where the disturbance to roots checks the plant's growth. The plants must then be hardened off gradually (removed from the protection of the greenhouse and introduced to the great outdoors) until they are ready to be planted out in late spring or early summer.

ABOVE: Propagating annuals is simple using a seedtray on a windowsill to provide light for strong growth.

HERBACEOUS PERENNIALS

When grown from seed these plants can flower well in their second season, but there are some which will take several years to reach flowering size. Cultivars and F_1 hybrids are unlikely to come true from seed, but species perennials will, although there may be variation in the depth of colour or leaf size. Sow the seed in spring or summer on a spare piece of ground or else under glass. Thin the seedlings as necessary and when the plants are large enough pot them up into 7.5 cm/3 in pots.

ABOVE: Propagating stocks of flowering plants from seed and cuttings is an inexpensive enterprise worth trying.

Cuttings

This is the easiest way to propagate many perennials, especially short-lived or half-hardy sorts. Shrubs are also easily propagated using cuttings. As with seed sowing, cuttings need to be kept moist, warm and provided with adequate light in order to thrive.

BASAL CUTTINGS

These types of cuttings are taken from herbaceous perennials and shrubs in early spring using new shoots, 5-7.5 cm/2-3 in long, which appear at the base of the plant. Using a sharp knife, cut the basal stem just below a leaf or joint. Dip the cut end into hormone-rooting powder or solution and briskly, but gently, shake off any excess. Put the cuttings into loose, sandy compost either in a cold frame or else evenly spaced around the edge of a 10 cm/4 in diameter pot. Cover the pot with a polythene bag or half of a clear, plastic soda water bottle to make a mini greenhouse – this will keep a moist atmosphere around the cuttings and keep them shaded as well. After a few weeks tug gently on a leaf; if the cutting resists the pull and stays firm in the compost, it has rooted. It can then be potted on, hardened off and finally planted out.

RIGHT: Some plants, such as this impatiens, will root easily in water. Geraniums will also root easily in water, as will willow, mint and many soft-stemmed, half-hardy ornamentals.

SOFT CUTTINGS

These cuttings are taken from non-flowering new shoots. Soft cuttings of shrubs and perennials can be taken in late summer. Remove new side shoots about 7.5-10 cm/3-4 in long and trim the end of the stem back to a pair of leaves, cutting cleanly just below the node, which is where the leaves attach to the stem. Remove all but the top pair of leaves and the growing point and proceed as for basal cuttings.

SEMI-RIPE CUTTINGS

These cuttings can be done using non-flowering shoots which have begun to ripen and turn woody at the base. They are also taken from shrubs and

ABOVE: Propagating clumps of herbaceous perennials can be done from autumn to early spring. Use pieces taken from the outer edge and discard the old woody centre.

perennials at the end of summer. These are pulled away from the main stem, taking a small heel of old bark at the base (which is why they are sometimes called heel cuttings). Treat as for soft cuttings.

ROOT CUTTINGS

These cuttings are used for a few plants such as oriental poppies and phlox. In late winter, cut sections of healthy root about 5–7.5 cm/2–3 in long; cut the bottom of the root (the end furthest from the top growth) at a slant to identify which way is up. Thick roots are potted vertically in compost, while thin roots are laid horizontally on a tray of compost. Cover with about 5 mm/¼ in of compost and put in a garden frame or cold green-house. Pot up the cuttings individually when new shoots appear and harden off gradually.

Division

This process is by far the most widely used method of propagation and is also good for rejuvenating old clumps of plants that are beginning to die out in the centre. Lift the plant clump and with two forks jammed back-to-back into the centre of the clump force the pieces apart by pulling the forks apart. Discard the old centre and trim and tidy the new sections taken from the outer sections. Plants can be divided in autumn or else in the spring.

BELOW: Snowdrops should be lifted and divided in the early spring after they have finished flowering and before the leaves have faded.

OFFSETS

These growths are nothing more than juvenile plants produced around the base of the parent. They can be cut or pulled away, often with a vestigial root, potted up and grown on before planting out into the garden.

Layering

This form of propagation is useful for some shrubby, woody plants and for some groundcover plants that have a tendency to root as they scramble over the ground. Choose a branch or stem that you can easily pull down to the soil, and then make a small slit where the shoots will touch the ground, but far enough from the growing tip that it will still be above ground when the layer is finished. Dust rooting powder in the wound or paint it with solution. Then peg this area down on the soil using a hairpin or piece of bent wire. Cover with a mixture of soil and potting compost, and when the new shoots appear the layer can be severed from the parent and moved to its new home.

PLANT DIRECTORY

THE FOLLOWING LIST OF PLANTS is compiled from the myriads of garden flowers you can grow. It is only a small selection, but is suitable for novice gardeners. In the entries below 'h' refers to plant height in good growing conditions, while 'p' indicates the planting distance between plants in groups.

Acanthus mollis
Bear's breeches
h 1–1.2 m/3–4 ft p 90 cm/3 ft
Summer-flowering herbaceous perennial with large, glossy green leaves and spikes of purple and white flower bracts in summer. Propagate by root division in early spring; self-sown plants are usually inferior. Does well in retentive soil and full sun, but will accept semi-shade. Acanthus is a good architectural plant to give structure to large borders, or as a single specimen plant or focal point. The roots are invasive and it can be difficult to eradicate, so be sure to put it where you know you want it. Cut faded flower stems almost to ground level and mulch the base of young plants to protect them from frost. Slug and snail damage can be a problem. *A. spinosus* has a finer, more deeply divided leaf.

Achillea filipendulina
Yarrow
h 1–1.2 m/3–4 ft p 45 cm/18 in
Herbaceous perennial, flowering from early summer to autumn. It has finely cut, lacy foliage and broad, flat flower heads in shades of ivory, cream, pink and yellow. Propagation is by division of established clumps in early spring. Prefers well-drained soil and full sun and will tolerate even the poorest soils. Achillea is long-lived and exceptionally hardy. Prolong flowering by regular dead-heading and stake the plants to prevent wind damage. Cut the stems to ground level at the end of autumn and mulch in late spring. Water only when necessary, but early in the day as overnight moisture encourages mildew and can damage flowers. 'Gold Plate' and 'Cloth of Gold' are good cultivars.

ABOVE: *Achillea filipendulina* '**Gold Plate**'.

RIGHT: A mixed summer border is a splendid sight. Here foxgloves, delphinium 'Pacific Hybrids' and *Paeonia lactiflora* 'Lady Alexandra Duff' give a good early summer show.

Achillea ptarmica

Sneezewort

h 45–60 cm/18 in–2 ft p 45 cm/18 in

Herbaceous perennial, flowering mid to late summer. It has insignificant, but aromatic foliage and clouds of white, button-headed flowers. Propagate by division in mid autumn or early spring. Does well in any well-drained soil, but has a tendency to be invasive in rich, moist soil. Cut faded plants to ground level in the autumn and divide annually to control its invasive character. 'The Pearl Group' of *A. ptarmica* and cultivars 'Perry's White' and 'Ballerina' are recommended.

Agapanthus

African lily

h 75 cm/30 in p 45 cm/18 in

Herbaceous perennial, flowering mid summer to early autumn, with broad, strap-like leaves and umbels of bright blue, tubular flowers. Propagate by division in mid to late spring. The plant makes crowns anchored in the soil by thick, fleshy roots; set the crowns no deeper than 5 cm/2 in. Can also be propagated by seed sown under glass during early spring, but will take several years to flower. Likes well-drained, but retentive soil in full sun; mulch annually in late spring to keep the soil moist. Cut faded flowering stems to ground level and in cold areas protect the plants from frost by covering the crowns with a thick straw mulch. This plant can also be container grown and moved indoors during winter. 'Headbourne Hybrids' are the most commonly seen cultivars.

ABOVE: Agapanthus 'Royal Blue' is another choice cultivar.

Ajuga reptans

Bugle

h 10 cm/4 in p 30–45 cm/12–18 in

Ground-covering herbaceous perennial, flowering early to mid summer, with dark mahogany-purple foliage and spikes of blue or white flowers. *A. reptans* will soon knit together to make a mat of leaf and flowers. Propagate by division throughout the year. Does best in moist, well-drained soil in sun or partial shade. It is prone to powdery mildew, but otherwise trouble free. Other cultivars include 'Variegata' with variegated foliage splashed cream and pink, 'Pink Surprise' with pink flowers or 'Alba' with stunning white flowers.

BELOW: *Ajuga reptans* is a good plant for foliage effect and ground cover.

Alchemilla mollis

Lady's mantle

h 45 cm/18 in p 60 cm/2 ft

Herbaceous perennial with foamy clusters of olive-gold flowers atop soft green, round leaves from early to mid summer. Propagate by division in autumn or early spring; self-sows freely, so transplanted seedlings can be

used to increase planting. Grown for its leaves as much as its flowers, *A. mollis* is good at the front of the border, where it can be allowed to sprawl, or among old roses as a groundcover. Long-lived it will form a sturdy, woody clump which can be difficult to divide. Dead-head to improve appearance and to avoid being overrun by seedlings.

ABOVE: The genus anemone is quite a large one and is usually low-growing, but the group of taller-growing forms, such as this *Anemone* x *hybrida,* offer attractive blooms in late summer and well into autumn.

Althaea rosea
Hollyhock
h 1.5-1.8 m/5-6 ft p 90 cm/3 ft
Hardy perennial, often grown as a biennial, flowering mid to late summer. Plants grown as annuals are less susceptible to rust disease than those grown as perennials; burn any plants that become infected. Propagate from seed sown indoors in late winter for spring planting or outdoors in late spring for planting out in early autumn; winter-sown plants should flower in the first year. *A. rosea* is the familiar, much-loved cottage garden plant with single or pompom-double flowers in every colour of the rainbow. Likes rich, well-drained soil in a sunny, sheltered position. Best planted in small groups at the back of the border or against a wall. Feed with liquid fertiliser as plants come into flower and water regularly during dry spells.

Alyssum saxatile
Gold dust
h 20-30 cm/8-12 in p 45 cm/18 in
Herbaceous perennial, flowering mid spring to early summer, which makes dusty green clumps of foliage covered in yellow flowers. Propagate from semi-ripe cuttings in late summer. Does well in freely drained soil in an open, sunny position. *A. saxatile* is a vigorous spreading perennial for the front of the early summer border, along paths or tumbling over low retaining walls. Free-flowering and long-lived; clip over plants at the end of the season to remove faded flowers. Generally trouble free.

Anemone x *hybrida*
Japanese anemone
h 90 cm/3 ft p 60 cm/2 ft
Herbaceous perennial, flowering late summer to mid autumn, with slender flower stalks bearing white or pink flowers, which tower over clumps of soft green foliage. Propagate by division in autumn or early spring. Prefers moist, well-drained soil in partial shade. 'September Charm' has soft pink, single flowers and a golden centre and 'Honorine Jobert' and 'Queen Charlotte' are especially recommended.

Anthemis tinctoria
Golden marguerite
h 90 cm/3 ft p 90 cm/3 ft

Herbaceous perennial, flowering mid summer, with bright yellow daisy flowers and frilly foliage. Propagate by division in mid autumn and plant in any well-drained soil in full sun. *A. tinctoria* is very free-flowering, so regular dead-heading will help to prolong the flowering into autumn, but otherwise it is trouble free. 'E C Buxton' is the cultivar to look for.

Antirrhinum
Snapdragon
h 23–30 cm/9–12 in p 23 cm/9 in

Half-hardy perennial, which is treated as an annual that flowers all summer. These plants are familiar cottage garden flowers which come in shades of pink, gold and red. Propagate from seed sown under glass in late winter or early spring. Plant out after all danger of frost in any well-drained soil in full sun. Antirrhinums are traditional bedding plants, good for the front of the border, or as a filling plant when used in small groups. Dead-head regularly to prolong flowering. Trouble free.

Aquilegia
Columbine; Granny's bonnet
h 90 cm/3 ft p 45 cm/18 in

Herbaceous perennial, flowering late spring to early summer, bearing clusters of flowers atop wiry stems in shades of cream, yellow, pink, red, crimson and blue. Propagate by division in autumn or early spring or by self-sown seedlings (which do not come true, so your colours may well become mixed). Likes well-drained, moist soil enriched with compost or

LEFT: The old border forms of aquilegias have the advantage of seldom requiring staking; the tall-stemmed, early summer flowering aquilegias are perfect for the cottage garden.

ABOVE: *Armeria maritima* is the most familiar armeria species and is a useful plant for the front of the border.

manure, in sun or partial shade. Aquilegias look best planted in bold clumps, so don't be in too much of a hurry to divide. Mildew can be a problem, so cut out faded flowering stems: leave the foliage. Columbine is somewhat poisonous if the leaves, seeds or flowers are eaten.

Armeria maritima
Thrift; Sea pink
h 10-15 cm/4-6 in p 23 cm/9 in
Evergreen perennial, flowering late spring to mid summer, which forms hummocks of narrow grassy leaves and umbels of white or pink flowers. Propagate by division in late summer or autumn. Suits any well-drained soil in full sun. *A. maritima* is a useful edging plant for the front of the border. Prolong flowering period by regular dead-heading.

Aster novae-belgii
Michaelmas daisy
h 30 cm-1.2 m/1-4 ft p 10-30 cm/4 in-1 ft (depending on variety)
Herbaceous perennial which flowers in early autumn. It makes clumps of erect stems covered in short, narrow leaves topped by clusters of little daisy-like flowers in shades of mauve, pink, red, purple and blue. Propagate by division from mid autumn to early spring. *A. novae-belgii*

31

requires well-drained soil in full sun. Water regularly, especially when in flower, dead-head routinely and support tall varieties. Cut the entire plant to ground level after flowering and divide every two to three years to maintain vigour. Mildew can be a problem, so spray with a fungicide at the first sign. Cultivars of *A. novae-angliae* are less prone to mildew so may be preferable, but the selection is not as extensive.

Astilbe
Astilbe
h 45-60 cm/18 in-2 ft p 60 cm/2 ft
Herbaceous perennial, flowering all summer, which makes clumps of deeply cut foliage and plumes of frothy flowers in shades of white, red, pink and mauve. Propagation is by division in early spring. Plant in deeply dug, well-manured, moist soil in light shade. 'Fanal' is one of the most richly coloured astilbes with foliage tinted reddish-brown, which deepens after flowering. Although astibles are generally long-lived perennials they are not invasive and flowering will lessen with the years. This effect can be offset with an annual spring mulch of well-rotted manure or compost. Water frequently in dry weather and divide mature clumps every three or four years. Cut out faded flower stems or else leave them to dry on the plants to make an attractive feature in the autumn border. Protect emerging growth from slugs and snails.

ABOVE: **The advantage of astilbes in a flower garden is that their strong stems require no staking and they bring vivid colour to dull gardens.**

Bellis perennis
Double daisy
h 15 cm/6 in p 15 cm/6 in
Biennial, flowering late spring to early summer, which makes clusters of soft green leaves and nosegay bunches of daisy flowers in shades of red, pink and white. Propagate from seed sown in nursery beds in early

LEFT: *Bellis perennis* **is a good filler plant for the spring when last year's bedding plants have been discarded.**

summer. Move plants to flowering positions in autumn. Does well in any soil in sun or partial shade. The garden hybrids are relatives of the common lawn daisy and are bright additions to the front of the border, the windowbox or as fill-in plants between more upright-growing plants. They require little care other than regular dead-heading to keep the plants tidy and to prolong the flowering period.

Brachyglottis spedenii 'Sunshine'
h 1–1.5 m/3–5 ft p 1.2 m/4 ft
Evergreen shrub, flowering early to mid summer, with sprays of bright yellow, daisy-like flowers. Propagation is from semi-ripe cuttings in early autumn. Plant in any well-drained, fertile soil in full sun. A good plant for exposed, windy gardens, this shrub is especially valued for its silvery grey foliage and mound-forming habit, which makes a good focal point in the border. Clip over regularly to remove faded flower stalks and to help the plant keep its neat shape.

Campanula glomerata 'Superba'
h 60 cm/2 ft p 45 cm/18 in
Herbaceous perennial, flowering mid to late summer, with umbels of bright violet-blue flowers atop erect stems. Propagate by division of its

RIGHT: *Brachyglottis spedenii* **is a well-regarded specimen as it can withstand harsh weather conditions, such as strong winds.**

creeping runners in early spring. Does well in any well-drained, moisture-retentive soil in full sun or light shade. It can become invasive, spreading by underground runners. The flowering is extended by secondary flowers in the leaf axils, and appear after the first flush of flowers. Cut faded stems to ground level after flowering has finished and protect young growth from slugs and snails.

Campanula medium
Canterbury bell
h 90 cm/3 ft p 30 cm/12 in
Biennial, flowering late spring to mid summer, with large cup-and-saucer flowers in white, pink and blue. Sow seed in nursery bed in early summer and plant out in early autumn for flowers the following summer.

LEFT: **The tall-growing species of campanula, such as** *Campanula medium* **shown here, will require staking as their stems are prone to flop in exposed postitions. Wire supports are recommended.**

RIGHT: *Centaurea cyanus* **are lovely, especially if small groups of the single colours are scattered among other plants in an informal flower garden.**

Alternatively, sow seed under glass in early spring for flowers that summer. Prefers well-drained soil in sun or partial shade. The tall flower stems will require staking in exposed positions, otherwise they are quite sturdy. Plants that have flowered in their first season may flower again the next year if cut to ground level after first flowering is over. Dead-head frequently and protect young plants from slug damage.

Centaurea cyanus
Cornflower
h 60 cm/2 ft p 30 cm/12 in
Hardy annual, which flowers early summer to autumn according to date of sowing. A favourite cottage garden flower in shades of blue, pink, red and white. Propagate from seed and sow in mild areas in early autumn for flowers the following summer or during early spring for flowers that summer. Self-sown seedlings can be transplanted to flowering positions during autumn. Likes well-drained soil in full sun. Dead-head to prolong flowering unless self-sown seedlings are wanted.

Cerastium tomentosum
Snow-in-summer
h to 15 cm/6 in p 30 cm/12 in
Herbaceous perennial, flowering late spring to early summer, which has clouds of snowy white flowers that cover the pale grey-green foliage. Propagate by division or from seed sown in spring. Plant in any reasonable soil in sun; it will even tolerate poor soils. When foliage dies back at the end of summer, it will look as though the mesh of creeping stems will never support another crop of flowers, but don't be taken in – instead use the opportunity to tidy the plant up and next season's flowers will be all the better. Use near the front of the border or against paths and edgings. Generally trouble free, but can be invasive so divide regularly.

Chrysanthemum, garden-spray type
Chrysanthemum
h 60 cm/2 ft p 45 cm/18 in
Half-hardy perennial, flowering late summer to mid autumn, which produces the familiar chrysanthemum flowers favoured in cottage gardens in shades of red, purple, yellow, gold and white. Propagates easily by division during autumn or from basal cuttings. Plant in well-drained soil, enriched with well-rotted compost, in full sun, and dead-head regularly. Although these spray chrysanthemums can overwinter in the garden you will get better plants if you raise fresh plants from cuttings. Lift the clumps at the end of autumn and overwinter them in a garden frame or greenhouse. From mid winter to early spring new shoots will appear at the base of the plants and these can be used to provide cuttings 7.5 cm/3 in long. Spray to protect against aphids and leaf miners during summer. Chrysanthemums can be a skin irritant.

Chrysanthemum maximum
Shasta daisy
h 75-90 cm/2 ft 6 in-3 ft p 60 cm/2 ft
Herbaceous perennial, flowering all summer, which makes clumps of dark green, glossy leaves and sprays of broad, white daisy flowers with a central egg-yolk yellow boss of stamens. Propagate by division in early spring. Plant in well-drained, enriched soil in an open position in either full sun or partial shade. Water regularly during dry weather and dead-head to encourage second flowering. Best blooms produced if the plants are divided every other year. You may have to spray against aphids and capsid bugs.

Clematis viticella hybrids
h to 1.2 m/4 ft p 2 m/6 ft
Hardy deciduous climbers, which flower mid summer to early autumn. Dark indigo blue, mauve, white and

BELOW: **The most familiar and widely grown climbers in the garden are clematis, but they do require careful pruning to remain in top condition.** *C. viticella* **'Abundance' is pictured here.**

shades in between give the flowers real distinction. Propagation is not easy, but layering or internodal cuttings can be achieved with patience. Plant in well-drained soil with plenty of well-rotted manure or compost and some lime dug into the planting site. Plant in full sun with roots in shade; this can be provided by screening the base of the plant with a piece of tiling or a slate roof tile. These small-flowered clematis look especially good if trained into small trees and shrubs in the mixed border or else allowed to trail over, around and through neighbouring plants. Mulch annually in spring with manure and water freely during the growing season. In spring cut all the previous season's growth to a pair of buds about 30 cm/12 in from the base of the plant.

Convallaria majalis
Lily of the valley
h 15 cm/6in p 15 cm/6 in
Herbaceous perennial, flowering mid spring to early summer, with sweetly scented, white nodding flowers. Propagate by division in late summer or autumn. Plant in moisture-retentive soil in partial shade or full sun. *C. majalis* is good for planting among shrubs and spreads gradually by creeping, underground roots. Plant the crowns just below the soil surface

BELOW: *Convallaria majalis* **are good for the front of the border because their lovely, light habit can be masked behind other plants.**

and firm well. Mulch generously each spring with well-rotted compost and water regularly during dry spells. Protect against slugs and snails, as they can destroy emerging shoots. **WARNING:** *C. majalis* is poisonous if the leaves, seeds or flowers are eaten.

Coreopsis verticillata
Threadleaf coreopsis
h 45-60 cm/18 in-2 ft p 45 cm/18 in
Herbaceous perennial, flowering from mid to late summer, with fine, deeply cut foliage and golden yellow flowers. Propagate by division in early spring or autumn and plant in full sun in well-drained, dry soil. *C. verticillata* is not invasive, so can and should be planted in small groups. Mulch lightly each spring and water only if the weather is dry. Cut faded flowering stems to ground level and cut back the entire plant at the end of the growing season. Divide every two or three years.

Crocosmia masoniorum
h 90 cm/3 ft p 30 cm/12 in
Herbaceous perennial growing from a corm and flowering from mid to late summer in shades of yellow, orange and red. Propagate by division in early spring and plant in any well-drained soil in full sun. *C. masoniorum* is dependably hardy in all but the coldest climates. Remove faded flower stalks, leaving foliage for winter protection; this can be tided up in early spring to make way for new growth. Generally trouble free.

Delphinium 'Pacific Hybrids'
h 1.5 m/5 ft p 90 cm/3 ft
Herbaceous perennial, flowering early to late summer, with tall, tapering flower stalks bearing blooms in shades of white, blue, powder-mauve and lilac. Propagate by division in autumn or early spring or from cuttings taken from new growth appearing at the base in early spring; be sure to dust all cut surfaces with fungicide. Likes limy, retentive soil enriched with well-rotted compost in full sun. The archetypal border plant with single or double flower spikes, delphiniums are short-lived and must be renewed frequently for good quality flowers. Plant in groups, firming the plants well into the planting holes. Put supports in place before the plants reach 30 cm/12 in and feed in spring to encourage strong growth. Cutting out the main flower spike, just below the lowest blooms, will encourage secondary flower stalks to develop. When these are 15 cm/6 in tall remove the faded flower stems and protect young plants from slugs and snails. Leaves that are deformed, blotched with yellow or stunted indicate virus disease – all infected plants must be destroyed. **WARNING:** Delphiniums are poisonous if the leaves, seeds or flowers are eaten.

ABOVE: **Delphiniums add a stately touch to any garden with their tall flower spikes. It is advisable, however, to remove the weaker shoots early in the season, leaving no more than four per plant.**

Dianthus barbatus
Sweet william
h 45 cm/18 in p 20–23 cm/8–9 in

Biennial which flowers early to mid summer in mixed shades of white, red and pink with a scent like cottage pinks. Propagate from seed sown in late spring and transplant during autumn for flowers the following summer; it also self-sows easily. Likes well-drained soil in full sun and is good for gardens on chalk. In ordinary soil it will benefit from the addition of lime.

Dianthus
Cottage pinks
h 30 cm/12 in p 30 cm/12 in

Evergreen perennial, flowering all summer, which makes a mound of spiky, grey foliage and sprays of sweetly scented flowers in shades of pink and white. Propagation is easy from cuttings of young side shoots taken after main flowering in mid summer and planted out that autumn or from layers made in early or late summer. Plant in well-drained, retentive soil (likes chalky soil) in full sun. Cottage pinks are good as edging plants or else planted in small groups amid old shrub roses or mid-height perennials. Pinch out the main stems of young plants in the first year to encourage side growths and a bushy shape. Old plants become woody and should be renewed every two or three years. 'Doris', 'Mrs Sinkins' and 'Dad's Favourite' are popular varieties.

Dicentra spectabilis
Bleeding heart
h 60 cm/2 ft p 45 cm/18 in

Herbaceous perennial, flowering late spring to early summer, which makes clumps of soft foliage and arching flower stems bearing dangling, heart-shaped flowers bi-coloured pink and white. Propagation is by division in autumn, but it must be done carefully as its roots are quite brittle. Prefers moist, well-drained soil in a sheltered position in sun or partial shade. One of the most graceful plants in the garden, it should be set individually among other plants that will succeed it in flower. It dies down naturally, so don't cut back the old growth, but do clear it away before the onset of winter. Once established, *D. spectabilis* is a long-lived plant; young growth, however, is liable to late frost damage, so protect with straw mulch. Also protect against slugs and snails.

ABOVE: *Dicentra spectabilis* is a good middle-of-the-road plant, which provides substance and colour in the flower garden. Its effect is highlighted with a framework of background and frontal plants.

Digitalis purpurea
Foxglove

h 1-1.5 m/3-5 ft p 45 cm/18 in
Biennial (sometimes perennial), flowering early to mid summer, with a spike of white or pink flowers emerging from a rosette of broad, tapering leaves. Propagation is from seed sown outdoors in late spring or early summer to flower the following year. Likes well-drained, retentive soil in sun or light shade. Plant *D. purpurea* in groups at the back of the border, so that fading foliage will be concealed. Encourage a second burst of flowers from side shoots by removing central flower spike when faded. Excelsior Hybrids Group is a good variety; look for the apricot-coloured strain for a different appeal. **WARNING:** Digitalis is poisonous if the leaves, seeds or flowers are eaten.

Doronicum plantagineum
Leopard's bane

h 45-60 cm/18 in-2 ft p 30 cm/12 in
Herbaceous perennial, flowering in early spring, which has glossy yellow flowers on erect, wiry stems and spreads slowly. Propagation is by division in late summer and it prefers moist soil in sun or partial shade. Cut the entire plant to ground level at the beginning of autumn. Spreads moderately quickly by means of shallow, creeping roots; can be invasive in rich soil.

ABOVE: Digitalis purpurea 'Excelsior' hybrids.

Echinops ritro
Globe thistle

h 1-1.2 m/3-4 ft p 45 cm/18 in
Herbaceous perennial, flowering mid summer to early autumn, which has spherical, thistle-like flowers that are a subtle shade of lavender-blue. It has very coarse foliage, which only looks good before flowering. Propagation is by division in autumn or spring, although it will seed itself liberally, which can be a nuisance, as its deeply delving root system makes it difficult to remove. Will do well in any soil as long as it is well drained and in full sun. Cut plant to ground level in the autumn. This plant is attractive to bees and butterflies.

BELOW: *Doronicum plantagineum* growing with *Arabis caucasica*.

Erigeron species and hybrids
Fleabane

h 10-45 cm/4-18 in p 45 cm/18 in
Herbaceous perennials, flowering mid to late summer, which have fluffy, daisy-like flowers in shades of pink, blue, mauve and white. Propagation is by division in early spring or autumn, although the low-growing *E. karvinskianus* will seed itself everywhere – hence the common name daisy-gone-crazy. Erigeron likes well-drained, retentive soil in full sun or partial

RIGHT: Daisy-like *Erigeron speciosus* (top) growing with *Oenothera tetragona*.

shade and is one of the easiest and most free-flowering border plants. Dead-head to prolong flowering and cut the plants to ground level at the end of autumn.

Eryngium bourgatii
h 45–60 cm/18 in–2 ft p 30 cm/12 in
Herbaceous perennial, which flowers mid to late summer. This plant is a member of the sea holly family and is one of the best coloured, silvery-blue plants for the garden. Propagation is by division or root cuttings in early spring. Plant in any well-drained soil in full sun; it will grow in the poorest soils. Cut the entire plant to ground level in autumn.

41

Eschscholzia californica
California poppy
h 7.5 cm/3 in p 10 cm/4 in
Hardy annual, which flowers all summer. Comes in shades of cream, yellow, orange, pink and red. Propagate from seed sown in late summer to flower in early summer the following year. Seed can also be sown in spring and this may be more reliable. Self-sows readily and should be encouraged to do so. Will grow in any soil that is dry and in full sun. One of the easiest annuals in the border, sow it with early spring bulbs so that it will be left undisturbed to flower and self-sow year after year.

Euphorbia species and hybrids
Euphorbia
h 10 cm-1.2 m/4 in-4 ft p 30 cm/12 in for larger sorts.
Herbaceous perennials, which flower from spring to mid summer. Most have bright, greenish-yellow bracts surrounding insignificant yellow flowers, but some, such as *E. griffithii* 'Dixter', have crimson-red bracts and bright yellow eyes. Propagation is from basal cuttings taken in mid spring. Euphorbias do well in any soil in full sun. *E. characacias* ssp. *wulfenii* is a popular specimen plant and *E. nicaeensis* has good, grey foliage.
WARNING: Euphorbias are poisonous if the leaves, seeds or flowers are eaten. Can also be a skin and eye irritant.

ABOVE: The advantage of *Euphorbia wulfenii*, besides their stunning, greenish petal-like bracts, is that they do well in almost any soil.

ABOVE: Fuchsia 'Swingtime'.

BELOW: The vibrant *Gaillardia* x *grandiflora*'Goblin'.

Fuchsia species and hybrids
Fuchsia
h to 1.2 m/4 ft p 1 m/3 ft

Deciduous shrubs, flowering late summer to mid autumn, which have double-frilled flowers in shades of pinkish-red, crimson, purple and white. Propagation is from semi-ripe cuttings in late summer or soft cuttings in spring. Fuchsias like a position in full sun or part shade in well-drained soil with added manure or compost. Water regularly and feed during spring growth. After flowering, cut the branches almost to ground level. Mulch against frost damage; if your region is particularly cold it is best to lift the plants and overwinter them in the greenhouse. Aphids can be a problem.

Gaillardia x *grandiflora*
Blanket flower
h 60-90 cm/2-3 ft p 20 cm/8 in

Herbaceous perennial, flowering all summer, which has bi-coloured flowers in shades of orange and red. Propagate from root cuttings or by division. Prefers full sun and sharply drained, light, sandy soil, as in heavy retentive soils the plant tends to be short-lived. Gaillardia has showy, daisy-like flowers and spreads steadily by creeping, rhizomatous roots. Tolerates heat and drought well. You can prolong flowering with regular dead-heading; cut the entire plant to ground level in autumn.

Galtonia candicans
Summer hyacinth
h 1-1.2 m/3-4 ft p 20 cm/8 in

Bulb, flowering late summer, which has tall spikes of dangling, white, bell-shaped flowers with a light perfume. Propagation is by division of offsets. Plant in full sun in any well-drained soil. This is a statuesque plant, which should be used among foliage plants, such as hostas or in groups at the back of a flower border. Plant the large bulbs at least 15 cm/6 in deep; they do not have to be lifted at the end of the season. Remove the faded flower stems, but leave the foliage to fade naturally, as it will feed the bulb.

Genista lydia
Rock broom
h 45-60 cm/18 in-2 ft p 30 cm/12 in

Deciduous shrub, flowering late spring to early summer, which has bright yellow flowers and a pleasing, mound-forming habit; the drooping branches are covered with sweet-scented flowers. Propagate from semi-ripe cuttings taken in late summer and plant in any dry soil in full sun. This is a good plant for chalky soils and is ideal for hot, sunny borders where the soil is light and dry. Requires little attention apart from feeding during the first year to encourage new growth.

Geranium species and hybrids
Cranesbill
h 45 cm/18 in p 60 cm/2 ft
Almost evergreen perennial, which flowers all summer through early autumn and bears pink flowers. Propagate by division after the plant has finished flowering. Will grow in most soils, but does best in retentive soil in full sun or partial shade. *G. endressii* is a good groundcover plant and its bright, dainty flowers are freely produced over a long season. 'A T Johnson', with its silvery-pink flowers and the bright pink 'Wargrave Pink' are good cultivars of this hardy geranium species. 'Johnson's Blue' flowers in early summer and is then covered with masses of violet-blue, saucer-shaped blooms. Cut all hardy geraniums to the ground when flowering is over and the first flush of foliage has faded; many will rejuvenate to give a second flowering period.

Geum chiloense
Avens
h 45–60 cm/18 in–2 ft p 45 cm/18 in
Herbaceous perennial, flowering all summer to early autumn, which has frilly, orange-red flowers dancing about on wiry stems. Propagate by division in early spring or from seed sown in spring or summer. Plant in well-drained soil in full sun or partial shade and dead-head regularly to encourage flowering. After flowering, cut back to within 15 cm/6 in from the ground and lift and divide every three or four years. Can be killed by a wet winter.

Gladiolus byzantinus
Gladiolus byzantinus
h 45–60 cm/18 in–2 ft p 10 cm/4 in
Hardy corm, flowering early summer, with wonderful magenta, gladiola-style blooms, which are much simpler than the showy hybrids used by florists. Propagate by lifting and separating small offsets from the parent corm, then grow on individually in pots to plant out in the second year. Likes well-drained, reasonably fertile soil in full sun. *G. byzantinus* is nicer on the eye and much easier to care for in the garden than the florist hybrids; it is also reliably hardy and appreciates being undisturbed. Lift and divide only when it becomes overcrowded. Not as susceptible to disease as the hybrids.

ABOVE: *Genista lydia* thrives best in the full sun and resents wet conditions.

BELOW: *Gladiolus byzantinus* is a reliably hardy plant for the border.

Gypsophila paniculata
Baby's breath
h 90 cm/3 ft p 60 cm/2 ft

Herbaceous perennial, which flowers all summer. This is the familiar filler flower used by florists, since the sprays of foamy, white flowers blend so well with other cut flowers; it behaves just as well in the border. Propagation is from basal cuttings taken in spring. Requires deeply dug, well-drained soil in full sun; plant where the deep-growing roots can be left undisturbed. Cut to ground level after flowering and protect young growth from slugs and snails. 'Bristol Fairy' is a common cultivar; 'Rosy Veil' has pink flowers. There is also an annual variety of gypsophila.

Helianthemum nummularium species and hybrids
Rock rose
h 15-25 cm/6-10 in p 30 cm/12 in

Evergreen sub-shrub, flowering all summer, which comes in shades of pink, white, red and yellow. Propagate from semi-ripe cuttings taken in late summer and plant in well-drained, reasonably fertile soil in full sun. The rock rose makes a pleasing sight at the front of the border, where it can be allowed to scatter its papery little flowers along pathways and edgings. Generally trouble free, but clip over occasionally to remove old, faded flowers and from time to time remove old wood. 'Wisley Primrose', 'Rhodanthe Carneum', 'The Bride' and 'Henfield Brilliant' are worthwhile plants to look for.

Helianthus decapetalus 'Loddon Gold'
h to 1.5 m/5 ft p 60 cm/2 ft

Hardy perennial and member of the sunflower family, which has the typical large, round, fully double yellow flowers. Propagate by division in autumn or early spring. Likes deeply dug, well-manured soil and full sun and needs staking to keep upright. Do note this cultivar can be invasive. 'Lemon Queen' is another hardy perennial sunflower cultivar to look for.

Hemerocallis hybrids
Day lily
h 60-90 cm/2-3 ft p 60 cm/2 ft

Herbaceous perennial, flowering in mid summer, which has funnel-shaped flowers in shades of yellow, red, cream and pink. Propagate by division in autumn or early spring. Likes any good soil that is not too dry and a place in full sun or partial shade. The common name derives from the fact that individual flowers last for only a single day, but there are many blooms on a stem and they open successively, so the plant has a long season. Mulch in spring and water regularly in dry weather. Divide when flowers become less abundant, usually every six or seven years. Don't overfeed as this encourages foliage at the expense of flowers. There are numerous named hybrids to choose from.

ABOVE: *Helianthus decapetalus* is a good supporting plant for the border with its double yellow flowers and bold leaves.

Heuchera sanguinea
Coral bells
h 45 cm/18 in p 23 cm/9 in

Evergreen perennial, flowering late spring through early summer, which has spikes of small, bell-shaped, reddish flowers. Propagate by division in late summer or early spring and plant crowns at least 2.5 cm/1 in below soil surface. Requires well-drained, light soil enriched with well-rotted manure or compost, in full sun or partial shade. Mulch each spring and dead-head regularly to encourage flowering. Although it is quite a hardy plant, emerging flower spikes may be damaged by late frosts. Old plants tend to become woody and push up out of the soil. Lift and divide when this occurs, usually every three or four years.

Hosta species and hybrids
Plantain lily
Herbaceous perennial. The mildly attractive flowers appear from mid to late summer, but it is the foliage that makes these plants so valuable in the garden. Hostas are available in an enormous range of sizes – from tiny groundcovers no more than 10 cm/4in tall to great elephant-eared plants nearly 1 m/3 ft tall; adjust planting distances according to the sort you choose. Propagation is by division in mid autumn or early spring and in mature plants you will probably have to slice through the roots with a sharp knife; younger plants can usually be teased apart to give a number of crowns. They like well-drained, moist soil enriched with well-rotted manure or compost in sun for best flowers (hot sun tends to scorch foliage) and shade for finest leaves. Hostas are long-lived and increase slowly, so plant where they can be left undisturbed. Water regularly during dry spells and protect from slugs and snails.

ABOVE: *Heuchera sanguinea.*

BELOW: **Because of the enormous range of new varieties available today, hostas are becoming one of the border plants of our time.**

Hydrangea macrophylla
Lacecap and mophead hydrangeas
h to 1.5 m/5 ft p 1.8 m/6 ft

Deciduous shrub, flowering mid to late summer, which has blue flower panicles, although on alkaline soil the flowers will be pinkish. Propagation is from semi-ripe cuttings in late summer. Likes well-drained, moist soil with well-rotted manure or compost dug in. Give a sheltered position in partial shade, but avoid east-facing aspects as morning sun on frosted growth could scorch tender shoots and cause winter damage. Remove old and damaged wood in early spring and dead-head in early autumn. 'Mariesii' is a lacecap with a lovely spreading habit; 'Ayesha' is a mophead with good, strong foliage and large flower heads.

Iberis sempervirens
Perennial candytuft
h 20-25 cm/8-10 in p 30 cm/12 in

Evergreen sub-shrub, flowering mid spring to early summer, with masses of clear white flowers over glossy, dark green leaves. Propagation is by cuttings taken in late summer to plant out the following spring in any well-drained soil in full sun. Reliably hardy, perennial candytuft quickly forms a spreading mat of flower and foliage, making it an effective path edging, or you can allow it to tumble over the edge of a retaining wall or along a path. Clip over after flowering to prevent the plants from becoming straggly.

Iris germanica
Bearded iris
h 90 cm/3 ft p 30cm/12 in

Evergreen perennial, flowering late spring to early summer. This species has deep blue flowers, but there are countless hybrids in shades of the darkest mahogany-red to pale ivory-white. Propagation is by division of the rhizomes after flowering. Cut the rhizomes into several individual pieces, each with a fan of healthy leaves and several roots. Trim leaves to 15 cm/6 in, sloping down from the centre to the sides. Plant with the top of the rhizome almost exposed and the roots firmly anchored in narrow trenches, made either side of the rhizome. Plant in well-drained soil with added compost in full sun. A familiar cottage garden flower, bearded iris makes a brief, but stunning show early in the season. When flowers fade, however, there is little of interest left, so it is a good idea to plant them at the back of the border where later-flowering plants will screen the fading foliage. Dead-head regularly to prevent seed production which would weaken the plant. Feed well in early spring, then mulch to conserve moisture in dry weather. Stem rot is the most common problem for this plant, and is caused by drought in spring and an over-rich soil. You will know the plant has stem rot when the outer leaves turn yellow and the rhizome becomes soft. If affected burn the plant and replace the surrounding soil with fresh compost. Also protect against slugs and snails. Irises are somewhat poisonous and can be a skin irritant.

ABOVE: Although stunning, *Iris germanica* do take several years to establish.

Kniphofia species and hybrids
Red hot poker; Torch lily
h 90cm-1.2 m/3-4 ft p 60-75 cm/2-2 ft 6 in

Evergreen perennial, which flowers early to mid summer when the tall flower spikes in brilliant shades of orange, red, yellow and cream emerge from the clumps of strappy, green foliage. Propagation is by division in early spring, using the young side growths as the new plants. Plant in well-drained, retentive – not waterlogged – soil with some added manure or compost in full sun. Mulch in spring and don't allow newly planted roots to dry out. Cut out old stems as flowers fade. Leave plants undisturbed to increase slowly; division may be needed after five years. Mulch around the base of the plants with straw for winter protection if you live in a severe frost area, or else tie the leaves together above the crowns. Kniphofia cross-breeds readily and there are literally hundreds of hybrids to choose from in many striking colours.

ABOVE: **Kniphofia's striking flowers make them useful for flower gardens, but they are quite exacting in their site requirements.**

Lathyrus odoratus
Sweet pea
h to 2.4 m/8 ft p 15 cm/6 in
Hardy annual, flowering all summer, which has the popular, sweetly scented flowers in shades of red, blue, pink and white. Propagation is from seed sown in mid autumn and it should be overwintered in a cold frame for planting out early to mid spring. Seed can also be sown in flowering positions in early to mid spring, but flowering will start a little later. To aid germination, nick each seed with a sharp knife and then soak overnight. Sweet peas are greedy feeders and like moist, deeply dug, loamy soil enriched with plenty of manure or compost in full sun. Mulch generously in spring with well-rotted manure to shade the roots. Grow in the border either trained up supports or else allow to scramble among the perennials and shrubs. Do note that it is essential to dead-head frequently and thoroughly for fresh flowers – the more you cut the more flowers will be produced.

BELOW: *Lavandula angustifolia.*

Lavandula angustifolia
Lavender
h from 30-90 cm/12 in-3 ft p 25 cm/10 in
Evergreen shrub, flowering mid to late summer, which bears spikes of soft, lavender-blue flowers. The planting distance mentioned above can be more for larger sorts. There are many named cultivars, but one of the best is 'Hidcote', as the whole plant is fragrant. Propagation is from semiripe cuttings in late summer. Lavender likes well-drained soil in full sun; it is good on chalky soils. Use small types of lavender as path edging or around patios where, as you brush past the plant, the fragrance will be released. To maintain a compact habit, clear away old flower stalks in autumn and in the early spring prune to new growth, taking care not to cut into the old wood as frost entering a pruned branch could cause it to die.

Liatris spicata
Gay feather
h 60-90 cm/2-3 ft p 30 cm/12 in
Herbaceous perennial, which flowers from mid to late summer and has spikes of dark lavender-blue flowers. Propagation is by division in early spring. Plant the roots at least 15 cm/6 in deep. Will self-sow, particularly in damp positions, but seedlings are unlikely to be true to type if from a named hybrid. Likes rich, well-drained, but moist soil in full sun. Water regularly in dry weather and cut out faded flower heads only – the leaves must be left to feed the roots. Long-lived but not invasive, it can be left undisturbed until overcrowded, when it should be divided.

Lilium named hybrids, trumpet-flowered
Lily
h 90 cm/3 ft p 15 cm/6 in
Hardy bulbs, which flower in early summer in shades of orange, pink, yellow and white. Propagation is from the individual scales of mature bulbs removed after flowering and planted in trays. Gently push the bottom edge of the scale into potting compost, cover the tray and leave in a cool, sheltered place. Small bulbs will form at the base of the scales. Pot on individually into 8 cm/3 in pots and plant out the following autumn. Likes deeply-dug soil with plenty of well-rotted manure or compost added; will not tolerate limy soils, but liberal amounts of peat dug in around the bulbs should help. In the border, place the lilies so that their

BELOW: *Lilium regale* makes a good subject for the centre or back of a mixed border.

stems and roots are shaded, but the flower heads are in sun. Plant in early autumn while soil is still warm, about 10-15 cm/4-6 in deep, placing a little grit or sand beneath each bulb on heavy soil, or use peat on light or alkaline soil. Select only fresh bulbs with strong, not withered, roots attached. If you are not able to plant immediately, plunge the bulbs into moist peat or sand. Remove spent flower heads and cut stems to the ground when leaves have faded. 'Enchantment', 'Green Dragon', 'Pink Perfection' and 'Mont Blanc' are cultivars to look for.

Lilium regale
Regal lily
h 1-1.2 m/3-4 ft p 15 cm/6 in
Hardy bulb, flowering mid summer, which has fragrant, trumpet-shaped, white flowers. This is a species lily that has the same requirements as the trumpet-flowered cultivars.

Lobelia cardinalis
h to 1 m/3 ft p 15 cm/6 in
Hardy perennial with dark, wine-red foliage and carmine flowers shaped like little butterflies, which appear in mid to late summer. Propagate by division in autumn or early spring. Requires rich, moisture-retentive soil in partial shade. Spreads slowly and should be watered regularly during dry spells. Cut out faded flowering stems.

Lobelia siphilitica
h 1 m/3 ft p 15 cm/6 in
Hardy perennial with soft green foliage and spikes of bright blue flowers, which appear in mid summer. Propagation is by division in autumn or early spring. Requires moisture-retentive soil and either full sun or partial shade. Can become invasive, so cut back to ground level after flowering.

ABOVE: Lobelias are one of the most useful of all hardy bedding plants, as they are truly at home as edging around borders. *Lobelia siphilitica* **is pictured here.**

Lonicera periclymenum 'Serotina'
Late Dutch honeysuckle
h to 4.5 m/15 ft p 3 m/10 ft
Deciduous climber, flowering mid to late summer, bearing clusters of reddish-purple, sweetly perfumed flowers, which fade to yellow-cream. Propagation is by layering in early autumn. For best flowers, plant in deeply dug, well-drained soil in full sun, but can also be grown in partial shade. Train up a trellis or on wires placed against a fence or wall, or through trees or shrubs. It does better when grown on its own, as competing for food and shade with the host plant will lessen flowering. After flowering cut hard back and then train new shoots as they emerge onto a support. This process must be done regularly or plants are likely to die

ABOVE: *Lychnis chalcedonica.*

BELOW: *Lychnis coronaria*'s **magenta flowers do stand out in the garden.**

ABOVE: *Lysimachia punctata* **is a strong grower, so must be looked after properly.**

out. The popular cultivar *L. periclymenum* 'Belgica' is similar, but flowers in early and mid summer.

Lupinus
Lupin
h 60-90 cm/2-3 ft p 45 cm/18 in
Herbaceous perennial, flowering late spring to early summer in mixed colours including red, yellow, blues and purples. Propagation is from basal cuttings taken in early spring or from seed sown outdoors in flowering positions, mid spring to early summer. Plant in any well-drained soil in full sun. Lupins have long been a favourite garden flower, even though the flowering season is short and the foliage quickly begins to look tatty. However, they can be camouflaged behind later-flowering plants. Mulch each spring with well-rotted manure or compost to keep roots cool during summer and to retain moisture. Water regularly in dry weather and dead-head routinely to promote a second show of flowers. Protect young shoots from slugs and snails. Do note that lupins are somewhat poisonous if the leaves, seeds or flowers are eaten.

Lychnis chalcedonica
Maltese cross
h 60-90 cm/2-3 ft p 30 cm/12 in
Herbaceous perennial, which flowers early summer and carries broad, flat heads of vermilion-red flowers atop erect stems. Propagation is by division in early spring or from self-sown seedlings, which can become a nuisance as it self-sows readily. Will be happy in any well-drained soil in full sun. It is long-lived with clumps increasing slowly; divide only when overcrowded. Dead-head regularly to promote second flowering and to prevent seed from forming.

Lychnis coronaria
Rose campion
h 60-90 cm/2-3 ft p 30 cm/12 in
Herbaceous perennial, flowering mid to late summer, which has grey foliage and lurid magenta flowers. Propagation is by division in early spring or after flowering and also from self-sown seedlings. *L. coronaria* is not fussy about soil, likes full sun and is good for dry, chalky soils. It is short-lived, but self-sows readily and you will find it wherever the seeds can reach. Cultivate as for *L. chalcedonica*.

Lysimachia punctata
Yellow loosestrife
h 60-90 cm/2-3 ft p 60 cm/2 ft
Herbaceous perennial, which flowers mid summer and bears spikes of bright yellow flowers. Propagation is by division in autumn. Plant in any

moisture-retentive soil in sun or partial shade. This plant is a strong grower and the creeping rhizomatous roots will soon choke weaker neighbours unless the plant is lifted and divided every few years. Remember to cut the stems to ground level after flowering.

Malva moschata
Musk mallow

h 1.2 m/4 ft p 60 cm/2 ft

Herbaceous perennial, flowering mid to late summer, with silvery-pink and finely cut foliage.

ABOVE: *Malva moschata* **with its silvery-pink foliage grows with** *Achillea ptarmica.*

Propagation is from basal cuttings taken in spring. Plant *M. moschata* in any well-drained soil in sun; it will also tolerate poor, light soils. Flowers abundantly over a long season, but this plant is not particularly long-lived, so should be sustained by routine propagation.

Matthiola incana
Brompton stock

h 60–75 cm/2–2 ft 6 in p 15–20 cm/6–8 in

Half-hardy annual, which flowers all summer and is available in mixed shades of white, pink, red and lavender. *M. incana* is much loved in cottage gardens for its sweetly scented spikes of pastel flowers. Propagate by sowing seed from late winter to early spring under glass; young plants should be ready to plant out in the spring after last frosts. Prefers well-drained, deeply dug soil in full sun, with the addition of some lime. Water frequently in dry weather and in exposed positions stake the plants.

Monarda didyma
Bergamot; bee balm; Oswego tea

h 60–90 cm/2–3 ft p 60 cm/2 ft

Herbaceous perennial, flowering mid to late summer, with many named cultivars available in shades of rose-pink fading to lavender and deep pur-

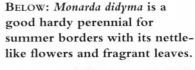

BELOW: *Monarda didyma* **is a good hardy perennial for summer borders with its nettle-like flowers and fragrant leaves.**

ple tints. This is a sweetly scented herb that deserves a place in every garden. Propagation is by division in early spring. Plant in any moisture-retentive soil, with plenty of added manure or compost, in full sun or partial shade. Develops rapidly into spreading clumps and can become straggly; regular division every two to three years improves its looks and helps to control its invasive habit. Many bergamots have the unfortunate tendency to mildew badly, but the strain named for the signs of the zodiac ('Aquarius', 'Capricorn', 'Libra' and 'Scorpio') seem to be free of this problem.

Nepeta x *faassenii*
Catmint
h 30-45 cm/12-18 in p 25 cm/10 in
Herbaceous perennial, flowering in early summer, with sprays of tiny, lavender-blue flowers and a romantic, grey foliage. Propagation is by division in spring or from self-sown seedlings. *N.* x *faassenii* requires well-drained soil in full sun and is a good plant for chalky soil. Invaluable for its long flowering period; it is good as an edging or as a filler between shrubby perennials and old roses. Cut hard back after flowering, which will encourage new growth and a second flush of flowers. 'Snowflake' has white flowers; 'Little Titch' is smaller. The cultivar 'Six Hills Giant' will spread to 1 m/3 ft – it's splendid, but untidy.

Nicotiana alata
Tobacco plant
h 60-90 cm/2-3 ft p 20 cm/8 in
Hardy perennial, which is usually grown as an annual. It flowers all summer to first frost and bears tubular flowers in shades of pink, rose, cream, white and lavender. Propagation is from seeds sown in spring or late summer. It will grow in any soil in full sun or partial shade. The plants self-sow freely and this can be a good way to allow them into the border; simply remove the ones you don't want. Makes tall, loosely branching plants which are fast-growing and free-flowering. 'Limelight' has lime green flowers, as does the species *N. langsdorfii*, which has dangling, tubular flowers. *N. sylvestris* is the magnificent wild tobacco, growing up to 1.5 m/5 ft tall, with brilliant white, highly fragrant flowers up to 15 cm/6 in long.

BELOW: *Nigella damascena* **is one of the loveliest and easiest of all hardy annuals to grow in the garden, and once they are there they stay.**

Nigella damascena
Love-in-a-mist
h 45 cm/18 in p 15 cm/6 in
Hardy annual, which flowers late spring to mid summer in blue, pink and white. Propagate by seed sown in flowering positions in early autumn for flowers the following year or from seed sown early to mid spring to flower that summer; once you have sown it, it will always be in the garden. Any good, well-drained soil in sun suits this old, cottage garden favourite. 'Persian Jewels' includes white and pink, as well as light and dark blue flowers. 'Miss Jekyll' is the popular sky-blue variety.

Paeonia species and cultivars
Peony
h to 1 m/3 ft p 60 cm/2 ft
Herbaceous perennial, which flowers in early summer. There is a huge range of colours and flower types – from single to

LEFT: Paeonia 'Pink Bowl of Beauty' is admired by many gardeners for its form, colour and perfume.

fully double and shades from white to the darkest wine red; some have golden stamens, in others the central boss is frilly white. Propagation is by division in mid to late autumn by lifting the clumps and cutting through the roots using a very sharp knife; each new piece should have at least two to three buds. Plant no deeper than the root was originally, in moisture-retentive, but well-drained soil with added compost in full sun or partial shade. Take care not to plant too deeply; the buds should be no more than 5 cm/2 in below the surface in heavy soils, otherwise 2.5 cm/1 in is deep enough. Clear away withered foliage at the end of the season, mulch with well-rotted manure or compost and fork in some bone meal around the plant, taking care to keep it clear of the crown. Protect emerging shoots from slugs and snails. Peonies are excellent cut flowers (pick while in bud) and provide autumn foliage.

BELOW: *Papaver orientale* is short lived, but is still one of the favourite garden plants.

Papaver orientale
Oriental poppy
h 90 cm/3 ft p 60 cm/2 ft
Herbaceous perennial, flowering late spring to early summer in flowers coloured white, scarlet red, raspberry pink, orange and even faded plum. Propagation is by division or by root cuttings in late summer. *P. orientale* is good for poor soils and borders in full sun. Plant crowns 8 cm/3 in deep and mulch lightly during the first winter. Oriental poppies leave a gap in the border when their

ABOVE: Given a hot summer petunias are one of the best half-hardy annuals; their trumpet flowers are very pleasing to the eye.

flowers and leaves have faded and been cut down, so use among later-flowering plants to disguise bare patches. 'Goliath' has huge, crimson-red flowers and 'Cedric Morris', 'Mrs Perry', 'Patty's Plum' and 'Raspberry Queen' are all worth looking for.

Petunia multiflora hybrids
h 23-30 cm/9-12 in p 15-23 cm/6-9 in
Half-hardy annual, flowering early summer to early autumn in shades of red, white, blue, purple and pink. Propagate from seed sown from mid winter to early spring in gentle heat to plant out after last frosts. Will grow in any good soil in full sun. Usually regarded as a container plant, the petunia is an invaluable border-filler plant, producing flowers over a long season. Dead-head regularly; if growth becomes too straggly, cut hard back and the plants will quickly regrow. Select varieties bred for weather resistance as rain and wind can damage plants.

Phlox paniculata
Border phlox
h 90 cm/3 ft p 45 cm/18 in
Herbaceous perennial, flowering mid summer, which has clusters of flowers in shades of white, mauve, pink and red. Propagation is from root cuttings done in late winter. Deeply dug, light, well-drained, but moist

LEFT: **Polygonums are known for their stout, angular stems and compact, cylindrical flower heads.**

soil, with added manure or compost in sun or partial shade suits this herbaceous perennial plant best. Mulch in spring to ensure the roots remain moist and water regularly in dry weather. Cut the entire plant down to 15 cm/6 in after flowering. Stem eelworm is a serious pest, causing stunted growth and shrivelled, distorted foliage. Destroy infected plants and don't replant phlox for at least three years.

Polygonum bistorta

Bistort

h 90 cm/3 ft p 45 cm/18 in

Herbaceous perennial, flowering late spring to early summer, which has dainty pokers of rosy-pink flowers above clumps of coarse foliage. Propagation is by division in autumn. Plant in moisture-retentive, but well-drained soil in partial shade and water regularly in hot, dry weather.

It spreads rapidly and can become invasive unless you lift and divide regularly. Cut to ground level after flowering and mulch in autumn.

Potentilla
Potentilla 'Yellow Queen'
h 30 cm/12 in p 20 cm/8 in
Herbaceous perennial, flowering all summer, bearing bright yellow flowers on wiry stems above strawberry look-alike foliage. Propagate by division in mid autumn to early spring. Likes well-drained soil in full sun. Free-flowering and trouble free. Water regularly in dry weather.

Rosa species and varieties
Roses: Old-fashioned; shrub and species
Old-fashioned roses predate the introduction of hybrid tea roses and cluster roses (floribundas), and are much better suited to growing among flower borders because of their relaxed habits of growth, attractive foliage and gentle flowers, colours and shapes, which blend more easily with herbaceous flowers and other shrubs. They vary in size from 60 cm/2 ft to over 1.5 m/5 ft and come in shades of white, pale shell pink and deep burgundy. Most have delicious perfumes. They will grow in any soil and benefit from an annual mulch of well-rotted manure or compost. The oldest types (some dating to the 16th century or earlier) will flower only once, in early to mid summer; later types will bloom continuously or be remontant – repeat-flowering. There are nurseries specialising in these roses, so obtain a catalogue to make your choice.

BELOW: *Rudbeckia fulgida*

Rudbeckia fulgida
Black-eyed Susan
h 45-60 cm/18 in-2 ft p 30 cm/12 in
Hardy perennial, flowering mid to late summer, which has large, daisy-like flowers with golden yellow petals around a black central domed boss. The stems are rigidly erect and the foliage is dark green and rather coarse. Propagate by division in autumn or early spring and plant in any well-drained, fertile soil in full sun. When flower size begins to decrease, it is time to lift and divide to rejuvenate the plantings. Water regularly during dry spells.

Salvia nemerosa
h 90 cm/3 ft p 45 cm/18 in
Herbaceous perennial, which flowers early to mid summer and bears spikes of flowers in shades of violet-purple, blue and lavender-pink. Propagate by

LEFT: *Salvia nemorosa.*

division in early spring and plant in any well-drained soil in full sun. It will also grow in poor, dry soils. *S. nemerosa* is long-lasting but not invasive. Dead-head regularly to prolong flowering and cut the entire plant to ground level after flowering. Mulch lightly in spring and in winter in very cold regions. 'Amethyst', 'May Night', 'East Friesland' and 'Rose Queen' are good cultivars to look for.

Santolina chamaecyparissus
Cotton lavender
h 45-60 cm/18 in-2 ft p 45 cm/18 in
Evergreen sub-shrub, flowering mid summer, with masses of tiny button flowers in bright yellow, but it is the aromatic foliage which is most valuable in the garden. Propagation is from semi-ripe cuttings in late summer. Plant in any well-drained soil in full sun. The finely divided grey leaves of *S. chamaecyparissus* make it ideal for use as edging or dot plants at the front of the border. It can also be trimmed to make a neat hedge, but flowers are produced only if the shrub is left unpruned. Flowering, however, makes the shrub become straggly, so

BELOW: **Prized for its silvery-grey foliage and bright flowers** *Santolina chamaecyparissus* **is a much-prized evergreen sub-shrub.**

ABOVE: *Saxifraga* x *urbium.*

prune hard in late spring. Cut back into old wood to encourage new growth from the base. Otherwise, remove the faded flower stems and clip the shrub over in mid autumn. The foliage is actually a herbal insecticide and renowned as a moth repellent; the old French word for the herb is *garde-robe.*

Saxifraga x *urbium*
London pride
h 30 cm/12 in p 25 cm/10 in
Evergreen perennial, flowering late spring, bearing sprays of pink flowers on wiry stems above the rosettes of dark green, tongue-shaped leaves. Propagation is from cuttings of growing tips in spring or by layering of runners. Plant in well-drained soil in sun. Remove faded flower stems and mulch in spring, as old plants become straggly and woody, and guard against slugs and snails, which damage foliage. 'Variegata' is a cultivar to look for, it has leaves splashed with vibrant yellow.

Sedum spectabile
Iceplant; Stonecrop
h 30-60 cm/12 in-2 ft p 45 cm/18 in
Herbaceous perennial, flowering late summer to first frost, bearing

RIGHT: Sedums are probably best known as houseplants, but there are also a number of species suitable to grow outdoors, such as this *Sedum spectabile,* which is long lived and easy to care for.

corymbs of rosy pink, dark red or white flowers. Propagation is by division in early spring or from stem cuttings in early summer. Plant in any well-drained, moisture-retentive soil in full sun. The honey-scented flowers are particularly attractive to butterflies. Long-lived, easy-to-care-for border plants, the flowers are good for drying and can be left to dry and bleach in situ to create winter interest in the garden, but remove them in the spring to tidy up. 'Herbstfreude' (syn. 'Autumn Joy'), 'Munstead' and 'Indian Chief' are good cultivars for the border.

Senecio speciosus 'Sunshine' (see *Brachyglottis spedenii* 'Sunshine')

Stachys byzantina
Lamb's ear
h 30-45 cm/12-18 in p 30 cm/1 ft

Evergreen perennial, flowering early to late summer, bearing spikes of pale mauve flowers. It is the pale grey, felted foliage, however, that this plant is valued for in the border. Propagation is by division in early spring. Plant in any well-drained soil in full sun or light shade. Superb ground-cover, especially with old roses, it spreads quickly and roots easily. Remove flower heads as they fade and clear away wilted foliage.

BELOW: *Stachys byzantina*'s spikes of pale mauve flowers stand out in any garden.

RIGHT: *Viola cornuta* '**Bambini mixed**'.

RIGHT: *Viola cornuta* '**Bambini mixed**'.

ABOVE: *Tanacetum coccineum*.

Tanacetum coccineum

h 60 cm/2 ft p 45 cm/18 in

Herbaceous perennial, which flowers late spring to early summer and sometimes again in late summer. Bears daisy-like flowers in bright shades of pinky rose, red and white. Propagation is by division in late summer or early autumn. Plant in well-drained, sandy loam with added compost in full sun or partial shade. Mulch in spring each year to help retain moisture during the growing season and water freely during dry spells. Prolong flowering by regular dead-heading and cut plants hard back after the first flowering to give a second show in late summer.

Tiarella cordifolia
Foam flower

h 20-25 cm/8-10 in p 20 cm/8 in

Herbaceous perennial, flowering late spring to mid summer, bearing frothy sprays of tiny, white flowers above attractive clusters of foliage. Propagation is by division in early autumn. Plant in moisture-retentive soil in partial shade. *T. cordifolia* is a good groundcover near the front of a shady border. Trouble free, just remove faded flower stalks.

Tradescantia x *andersoniana*
Spiderwort

h 45-60 cm/18 in-2 ft p 38 cm/15 in

Herbaceous perennial, which flowers most of the summer and bears interesting, butterfly-like flowers in shades of purple, blue and white. Propagation is by division in spring; plant in moisture-retentive soil in full sun or shade. Spiderwort will grow just about anywhere, provided it is relatively moist. Avoid planting in too fertile soil, as it will quickly colonise by creeping rhizomatous roots. It also roots wherever the jointed stems touch the soil, and so can be increased by layering.

Viola cornuta
Horned violet
h 10-23 cm/4-9 in p 20 cm/8 in
Hardy perennial, which flowers early to mid summer and bears masses of small, violet-blue flowers. Propagate by division in mid spring or by basal cuttings in mid summer; also self-sows readily. Likes cool, moisture-retentive soil in partial shade or sun. You must water regularly during dry spells and dead-head by clipping over the plants to achieve continuous flowering. Makes a good groundcover among shrubs.

Viola x *wittrockiana*
Pansy
h 15-23 cm/6-9 in
p 20 cm/8 in
Perennial best treated as a biennial or annual, which flowers all summer in a rainbow cascade of colours. Propagate by sowing seed in mid summer in the greenhouse and prick out into an open seed bed when large enough to handle. Keep moist. Plant out in the autumn to flower from early summer the following year. Can also be sown in late winter or early spring under glass

ABOVE: *Viola* x *wittrockiana* **'Reveille Cassis'.**

and planted out in late spring to flower the same year. Pansies like well-drained, moist soil, with added manure or compost, in sun or partial shade. Plant in bold masses at the front of the border and dead-head to keep them flowering all summer. Water regularly in dry weather.

Yucca filamentosa
Adam's needle
h 90 cm-1.2 m/3-4 ft p 90 cm/3 ft
Evergreen shrub, flowering mid to late summer, bearing a single, huge spear of bell-shaped flowers every two to three years. The flowers have a strong perfume and the plant, with its sword-like foliage, makes a bold statement in mixed plantings. Propagation is from offsets removed in spring and planted on in any well-drained soil in full sun. If planted in groups in the border, stagger the age of the plants to ensure continuous flowering over the years. It is a durable plant requiring little attention, except regular watering in dry weather.

INDEX

(References to photographs are indicated by *italics.*)

Picture Acknowledgements
The work of the following photographers has been used:
David Askham: 24, 57; Lynne Brotchie: 18(t), 27, 38, 54(t); Linda Burgess, 51(t); Chris Burrows: 23, 43(t), 53, 61(t), 62; Rex Butcher: 13(t); Brian Carter: 19(b), 29, 31, 43(b), 44(t), 45, 46(t), 55, 61(b); Densey Clyne: 32(b), 48(t); Ron Evans: 7, 33, 58(t); Christopher Fairweather: 42; Nigel Francis: 6; John Glover: ii, 10(b), 11(b), 26, 36, 39, 52(t), 59(t); Sunniva Harte: 41, 50, 54(b); Marijke Heuff: 10(t), 11(t), 40(t), 52(b), 56; Neil Holmes: 30, 32(t), 51(c), 58(b); Michael Howes: 8; Noel Kavanagh: 34; Lamontagne: 16(t), 35; Jane Legate: 16(b), 18(b), 25; Mayer/LeScanff: i, 20, 22(b); Zara McCalmont: 14, 22(t); Clive Nichols: 59(b); Jerry Pavia: 48(b), 60; Howard Rice: 13(b), 19(t); Gary Rogers: 21 and jacket; David Russell: 37, 44(b); J S Sira: 15, 28(t), 47, 51(b); Brigitte Thomas: 12; Juliette Wade: 9, 17; Mel Watson: 49; Didier Willery: 40(b), 46(b); Steven Wooster: 28(b).

The following gardens were photographed:
The Dillon's Garden, Dublin, Ireland: ii; Orchards Garden: 7; Upperwood Hill farm: 10(b); The Priona Garden: 11(t); St Agnes College, Newmarket, England: 14; Bassingbones, Buckinghamshire, England: 17; Lackham College Gardens: 57; Hampton Court Garden show, 1994: 27, 38; Audrey Flower's Garden, Hampton 1994: 54(t);
Edinburgh Botanic Gardens: 40(t); Little Hutchings, Sussex, England: 41; Merriments Garden, Sussex, England: 50.